by Anita Stasson

Consultant:
Beth Gambro
Reading Specialist
Yorkville, Illinois

Contents

Car to Jar 2

Key Words in the *-ar* Family 16

Index 16

About the Author 16

Minneapolis, Minnesota

Car to Jar

I see a toy **car**.

I see a gold **star**.

I see some black **tar**.

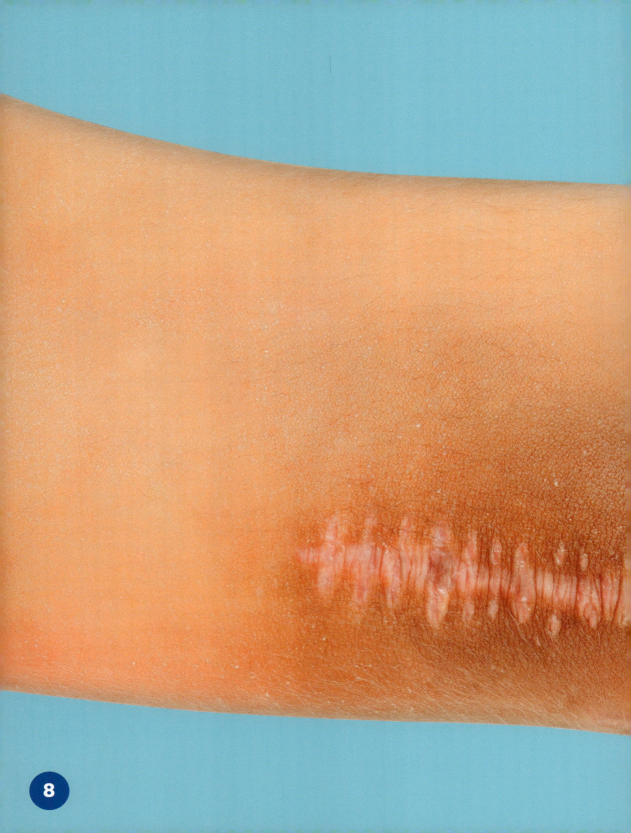

I see a big **scar**.

I see a candy **bar**.

I see a blue **guitar**.

I see a bug **jar**.

Key Words in the -ar Family

bar

car

guitar

jar

scar

star

tar

Other **-ar** Words: **char, far, spar**

Index

bar 11
car 2
guitar 12
jar 15
scar 9
star 5
tar 7

About the Author

Anita Stasson lives in Minnesota. She thinks rhyming is the bee's knees.

Teaching Tips

Before Reading
- ✔ Introduce rhyming words and the **–ar** word family to readers.
- ✔ Guide readers on a picture walk through the text by asking them to name the things shown.
- ✔ Discuss book structure by showing children where text will appear consistently on pages. Highlight the supportive pattern of the book.

During Reading
- ✔ Encourage readers to read with their finger and point to each word as it is read. Stop periodically to ask children to point to a specific word in the text.
- ✔ When encountering unknown words, prompt readers with encouraging cues such as:
  - **Does that word look like a word you already know?**
  - **Does it rhyme with another word you have already read?**

After Reading
- ✔ Write the key words on index cards.
  - **Have readers match them to pictures in the book.**
- ✔ Ask readers to identify their favorite page in the book. Have them read that page aloud.
- ✔ Choose an **–ar** word. Ask children to pick a word that rhymes with it.
- ✔ Ask children to create their own rhymes using **–ar** words. Encourage them to use the same pattern found in the book.

Credits: Cover, © Alexei Sysoev/Adobe Stock, © Mariyana M/Shutterstock, © alslutsky/Shutterstock, and © skydie/Shutterstock; 2–3, © Oez/Shutterstock; 4–5, © TheFarAwayKingdom/Shutterstock; 6–7, © milanfoto/iStock; 8–9, © energyy/iStock; 10–11, © Sezeryadigar/iStock; 12–13, © prill/iStock; 14–15, © Phodo Design/Adobe Stock and © Kuttelvaserova Stuchelova/Shutterstock; 16T (L to R), © Sezeryadigar/iStock, © Oez/Shutterstock, © prill/iStock, and © Phodo Design/Adobe Stock; and 16B (L to R), © energyy/iStock, © TheFarAwayKingdom/Shutterstock, and © milanfoto/iStock.

Bearport Publishing Company Product Development Team
President: Jen Jenson; Director of Product Development: Spencer Brinker; Managing Editor: Allison Juda; Associate Editor: Naomi Reich; Senior Designer: Colin O'Dea; Associate Designer: Elena Klinkner; Associate Designer: Kayla Eggert; Product Development Specialist: Anita Stasson

Library of Congress Cataloging-in-Publication Data is available at www.loc.gov or upon request from the publisher.
ISBN: 979-8-88822-047-4 (hardcover); ISBN: 979-8-88822-241-6 (paperback); ISBN: 979-8-88822-362-8 (ebook)

Copyright © 2024 Bearport Publishing Company. All rights reserved.
No part of this publication may be reproduced in whole or in part, stored in any retrieval system, or transmitted in any form or by any means, electronic, mechanical, photocopying, recording, or otherwise, without written permission from the publisher. For more information, write to Bearport Publishing, 5357 Penn Avenue South, Minneapolis, MN 55419.